A RENAISSANCE ALPHABET

A RENAISSANCE ALPHABET

IL PERFETTO SCRITTORE, PARTE SECONDA

GIOVAN FRANCESCO CRESCI

with an introduction by

DONALD M. ANDERSON

THE UNIVERSITY OF WISCONSIN PRESS

Madison, Milwaukee, & London

Published 1971
The University of Wisconsin Press
Box 1379, Madison, Wisconsin 53701

The University of Wisconsin Press, Ltd.
27–29 Whitfield Street, London, W.1

First printing

Printed in the United States of America

ISBN 0–299–05761–5
LC 77–121765

INTRODUCTION: *CRESCI AND HIS CAPITAL ALPHABETS*

The elegant letters reproduced here were conceived and drawn by Giovan Francesco Cresci, and were the heart of *parte seconda* of the writing manual, *Il perfetto scrittore*, that Cresci published in Rome in 1570. Cresci's organization of *Il perfetto scrittore* permits this presentation of Roman capital letters for the work was in effect two books bound together. Part one ends on a left-hand page with this colophon: *STAMPATO IN ROMA/in casa del proprio autore & intaglia-/to per l'Eccellente intagliator/M. Francesco Aure/ri da Crema.* Opposite this a new title page introduces part two, with fourteen lines of type within a typically ornamented copper intaglio border, beginning: *IL PERFETTO SCRITTORE/DI M. GIO. FRANCES-CO CRESCI/CITTADINO MELANESE.* The next four lines describe the content: "wherein contained the true forms of the ancient Roman capitals necessary to the art of the perfect writer. With his own discourse."

The text that follows is addressed to Pope Pius V, on one right-hand page and set in italic types. In turn, there come a two-page dedication to Cardinal Salviati, Cresci's sponsor and an official to the Holy See, set in Roman types, and Cresci's discourse on a subject of lesser interest, set in italic types.

The pertinent text in the front matter of the second part of *Il perfetto scrittore* is of course that which expresses Cresci's views on the letters reproduced here, the *Discorso delle Maiuscole antiche Romane.* This treatise on the ancient Roman capital letters is printed here, with a translation by Robert J. Rodini. Professor Rodini, whose principal area of interest is sixteenth-century Italian literature, thinks that Cresci's style is not of the first class, and he has rearranged some of the author's sentences with a view to improving the sense and flow of the language.

It is now just 400 years since *Il perfetto scrittore* first appeared in Rome. And yet there is little knowledge about Cresci's life that adds significantly to that which can be deduced from his published works. As indicated in the title pages of *Il perfetto scrittore*, Cresci was a citizen of Milan. His family was well connected. A. S. Osley, working from the few clues available, believes the date of Cresci's birth was near 1534. A youthful Cresci appeared in Rome early in the 1550s and was appointed scriptor to the Vatican library in 1556; a second appointment with the Sistine Chapel came four years later. In these appointments Cresci no doubt sharpened his skills in the Chancery cursive style of writing in development before 1500 and featured in the writing manuals of Ludovico degli Arrighi, Giovanantonio Tagliente, Giovanbattista Palatino, and others. A good many plates in Cresci's first writing manual were devoted to the *cancellaresca*, and his reputation as an innovator in this form brought him into a rather bitter word confrontation with an older expert, Palatino—but that is another story.

Even now, as Cresci emerges as a leading writing master of the sixteenth century, it is very doubtful if we would be concerned with what he said were it not for the disciplined workmanship of the man credited in the colophon to part one of *Il perfetto scrittore*. This was Francesco Aureri of Crema. Aureri, whose name is Spanish, cut the blocks for both of Cresci's important writing manuals, *Essemplare di più sorti lettere* and *Il perfetto scrittore*. Aureri was indeed the excellent *intagliator*, serving Cresci as Jean de Vingle had served Juan de Yciar in the latter's superb writing manual *Arte subtilissima*, published in Saragossa in 1550. But if Aureri's skills were gracefully acknowledged by Cresci and can be admired today in the fine letters of this edition, it must be noted that Aureri did not initiate structure or detail. The correspondence between the visual content of the letters Cresci designed and what he said about them seems to provide an assurance that Aureri cut what Cresci drew. Still, this aside, the collaboration itself was an act of elegance.

The first of Cresci's manuals, *Essemplare di più sorti lettere*, was published in Rome in 1560. If, as seems reasonable, the 53 plates of *Essemplare* were in preparation for a year or two, Cresci might have been 24 or 25 years of age when his first Roman capital alphabet was drawn and converted to plates. This alphabet appears at the end of *Essemplare*, 24 letters, with Y appearing in two versions. Three blocks prepared by Aureri for the presentation of Cresci's first interpretation of the ancient Roman capitals are reproduced here for purposes of study and comparison (Fig. 3). Letters appear white on a dark field, which means that Aureri cut them intaglio, below the surface of end-grain slabs of wood. This method of letter reproduction and its hazards were no doubt the principal consideration in Cresci's decision to print the capital letter blocks in *Il perfetto scrittore* twice. Some brief explanation of Renaissance printing techniques will illuminate the problem Cresci confronted.

In Europe letters and illustrations were combined in relief-cut wood blocks before the use of metal types—the so-called block book. Gutenberg's method of letter production in relief metal, and the spread of it, had led to the death of the block book by about 1480, but large initial letters, decorative borders, and illustrated material of all kinds continued to be cut in wood and used with metal types.

The method of the block book was revived, however, in the first writing manual, *La operina* by Ludovico degli Arrighi, published in Rome in 1522. The whole of this manual was cut on wood blocks without the aid of metal types. An addition to this, Arrighi's *Il modo de temperare le penne*, was published in 1523, with the essay material accompanying the wood-cut writing specimens set in italic types of Arrighi's design. After 1523 writing manuals were produced in a combination of wood-cut and metal type relief images, until Giu-

liantonio Hercolani issued his *Lo scrittor' utile* in 1574 with writing specimens cut intaglio in copper plates.

The intaglio wood method employed by Cresci and Aureri in Cresci's capital alphabets of 1560 and 1570, with letters reading white on a black field, is first observed in writing manuals in Arrighi's *Operina*, where in a single usage it appears in a fine little colophon (Fig. 1). In *Il modo de temperare le penne* Arrighi's usage of the engraved method increased to eight examples, with several alphabetic

Fig. 1. Arrighi's colophon from *La operina*, 1522.
The Newberry Library, Chicago

presentations seen white on black, notably two blocks presenting Arrighi's version of proper Roman capitals. These are reproduced here (Fig. 2) to establish Cresci's models in method of alphabetic presentation, and also to introduce one of several letter traditions that Cresci was heir to.

As we may see in the reproduction of six of Cresci's 1560 letters, his first rendition of the Roman capitals does indeed communicate power in graphic content. They are sturdy letters, strong and hand-

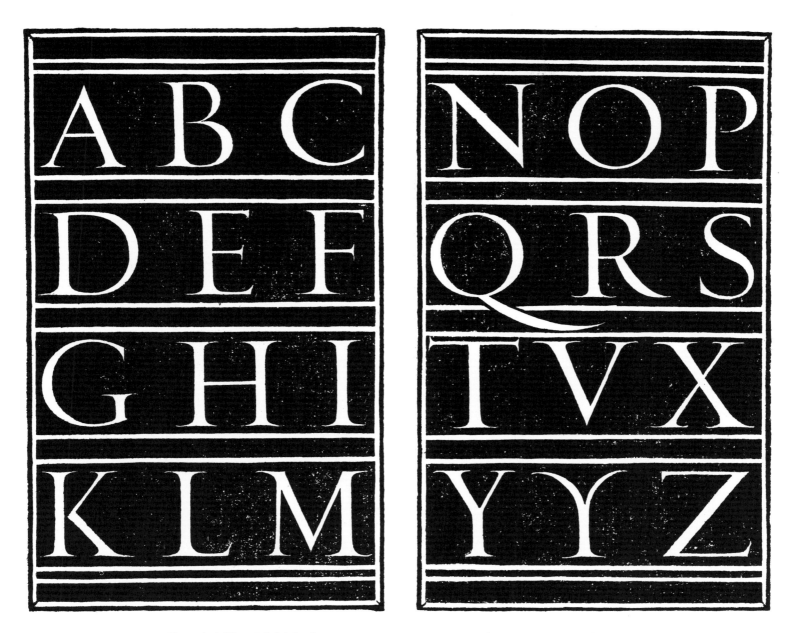

Fig. 2. Arrighi's capital alphabet from *Il modo de temperare le penne*, 1523. The Newberry Library, Chicago.

Fig. 3. Three alphabetic plates from *Essemplare di più sorti lettere*, 1560. The Newberry Library, Chicago. (The Newberry Library copy of *Essemplare* lacks the YZ leaf. The version here is courtesy John Ryder, London.)

some, with a proportion of one to eight in stem width to height. Serifs are very generous and end in a little calligraphic curl. These flourished serifs are attached to stems which are rigidly parallel, and these two characteristics give Cresci's 1560 alphabet a unique character. In Cresci's treatise on the Roman letters that precedes the plates of *Essemplare*, tribute was paid to ancient Latin inscription capitals for exemplifying "the origin and basis of perfect writing." In the design of B, Cresci cited the example to be observed in "that fine inscription at the foot of Trajan's column." Cresci had in fact at that early age studied the ancient forms quite carefully, and the curve and bowl formations fairly reflect Roman inscription calligraphy. The pleasant assymetry of the counter forms of the Roman B are also seen in Cresci's B.

Cresci held fine appointments and he was skillful. He broke no new ground in modesty, but exemplars are few in that era. Rather, he reflected his times in Cresci on Cresci, stating that the simple truth concerning the ancient letters could be found in his essay in *Essemplare*, in which he places himself as that authority who explains the true and fixed rules of the ancient capitals in spite of the enmity of rivals who seek "to bite me with the tooth of envy." Thus in his early career Cresci had already attracted real and imaginary adversaries, and acquired that arrogance which so marked the utterance of later writing masters that Isaac D'Israeli paused to dissect them in a choice essay in *Curiosities of Literature*.

Cresci undoubtedly overstated his case in the 1560 manual, and the 1560 capitals contain many features which differ from the calligraphy of the Empire stones. His treatment of serifs, for instance, varies from the older letters, and there seems no comparison between the letters of *Essemplare* and the Roman inscriptions available to Cresci that could give a paleographer the palpitations of discovery. Nor does it seem likely that the Cresci alphabet of 1560 can be derived from inscription styles of the Renaissance, which, particularly after Alberti's effort on the façade of Santa Maria Novello in Florence in 1456, evince the clear imprint of the Empire letter in skilled imitation. This may be seen in our reproduction of the inscription on the tomb of Cardinal Jacopo Sclafenato, who died in 1497 (Fig. 4). Sclafenato's inscription was produced by the workshop of Andrea Bregno, who in the last third of the fifteenth century was influential in the use of the Imperial inscription form. It should be noted that the elimination of the medieval letter and the acceptance of the Trajan model was complete in Rome by 1500, long before Cresci drew his *Essemplare* capitals.

It is quite likely that the vigorous letters in *Essemplare* are only in part derived from inscription sources. The serif treatment is very much like that seen in Arrighi's capitals. Perhaps this earlier Vatican scribe suggested, in the letters of *Il modo de temperare le penne*, how Cresci might draw his own letters in his own way, for they are unique.

Of the various essays in *Essemplare*, that part devoted to the capital letters was a defense of Cresci's own views in deriving his style from that of the ancient letters and at the same time an attack on those who sought to interpret these honored letters through compass and rule. The letters and the essay in *Il perfetto scrittore* may be said to complete his views on the subject.

Cresci did not like compass derivations, and in so stating he dismissed the entire log of respected humanistic lore on ancient decrees of proper proportion. Interest in these matters had been prefaced by a return of ancient mathematics to Europe through translations of Arabic manuscripts into Latin in the twelfth century. Humanistic scholarship of the fifteenth century became deeply involved in Euclid and in arithmetical operations and algebraic methods. A part of this, peripheral perhaps to the advancement of arithmetic, geometry, and algebra in their purest propositions, was that part of descriptive geometry called perspective. First outlined in the classic work of Vitruvius Pollio, *De architectura*, the subject was again taken up by Leon Battista Alberti, who presented his first views on perspective in 1446, in *Della pictura*, with his pyramid of rays running from the eye to the object and intersecting an intermediate picture plane, as it is called in our day. *De prospectiva pingendi* (ca. 1478), Piero della Francesca's more detailed work, went into the tedious documentation of rules and also offered brilliant graphic representations, including strange projections of column capitals and human heads. There followed the skilled projections by Albrecht Dürer, of which the circular helix or spiral staircase is of classical order. This background helps to explain the tools and methods of drawing available to those who constructed Roman capitals in the Renaissance. In matters of proportion these men mainly relied on the measures out-

lined by Vitruvius, the talented Greek practitioner of Roman engineering, architecture, and what have you.

No doubt a central part of the holy science of Vitruvius in the Renaissance times derived from Euclid, in the concept of the square inscribed in a circle and the circle inscribed in the square. Apparently Vitruvius added certain elements, derived from older sources, that impressed a number of Renaissance scholars and artists. This is most evident in the famous drawing by Leonardo da Vinci deriving from *De architectura*, Book III, Chapter I: "Then again, in the human body the central point is naturally the navel. For if a man be placed on his

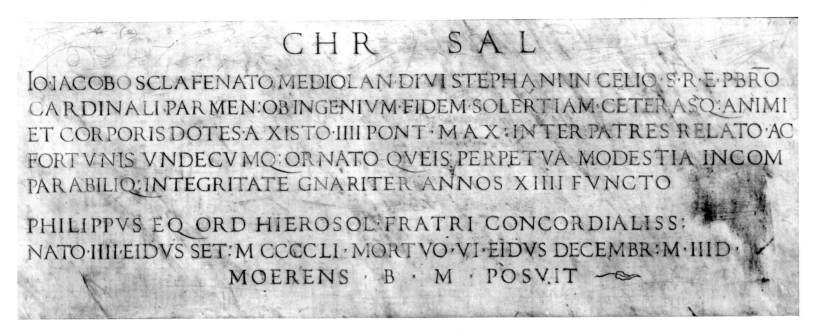

Fig. 4. Letters from the tomb of Cardinal Sclafenati, in Rome ca. 1497. Alinari photograph.

back, with his hands and feet extended, and a pair of compasses centered at his navel, the fingers and toes of his two hands and feet will touch the circumference of a circle described therefrom."

These ideas from Vitruvius, a practical man, invaded the thinking of later practical men, who included them in ideas concerning the construction of Roman letters. This particular theme is an invading premise in many of the constructed alphabets of the Renaissance. For example, the writing manual published in 1526 by Giovam Baptista Verini, his *Luminario*, featured a representation of the Vitruvius figure (Fig. 5) that should tempt a diagnostician.

The first Renaissance treatise which attempted to relate Roman capitals to classical lore was created by Felice Feliciano in about 1460. This alphabet exists in the Vatican Library (Ms. Vat. lat. 6852) and was not printed in its own time. Feliciano's manuscript rationale appears beneath each letter. His version of the Roman capitals used a main stroke of one to ten in stem width to height. This undoubtedly stems from Vitruvius too, who remarked that the Greeks considered it a perfect number: "Again, while ten is naturally perfect, as being made up of the fingers of the two palms, Plato also held that this number was perfect because ten is composed of the individual units, called by the Greeks *monades*. But as soon as eleven or twelve is reached, the numbers, being excessive, cannot be perfect until they come to ten for the second time."

Of course, this particular measurement was available from ancient inscription capitals *in situ*, and Feliciano had considerable experience in copying the ancient letters. One instance of his participation is recorded in "*Jubilatio*," quoted in Paul Kristeller's *Andrea Mantegna*, wherein the two friends, Feliciano and Mantegna, toured the shores of Lago Garda with companions, obtaining 22 inscription copies before or during festivities of lesser scholarship. Feliciano said that he had measured the ancient letters and no doubt he had. The persistence of the mythology of Vitruvius in the constructed alphabets of the Renaissance suggests that having indeed measured the ancient letters

Feliciano and others found only a happy confirmation of what Vitruvius had said, whereas in reality the pragmatic brush calligraphy of Roman inscriptions seems to have developed without the benefit of Vitruvius or any other theoretician on proper proportion. Feliciano's alphabet and text is a marvelous document, because the author was

Fig. 5. Vitruvius figure from Verini's *Luminario*, 1526. Biblioteca Nazionale Centrale, Florence.

not sufficiently skilled in writing (or drawing, for that matter) to have hidden the fact that the doctrine of Vitruvius and what he observed around Lago Garda and otherwere were in conflict. His pitiable attempts to reconcile the two views should have warned more learned men who failed the same test.

The format which Feliciano initiated for the explanation of the ancient Roman capitals was the square and inscribed circle with diagonals from the corners of the square. The diagonals made by connecting the corners of the square were not of much use to Feliciano but he did use one of them to establish the stress angles of O and Q—a decision which should have astonished any *marmorarius* of the day.

One consistently weak part of Feliciano's theory resides in his thinned transversals. It is hardly possible that he could have observed this feature in the horizontal strokes in ancient inscriptions, and so it must be assumed that these too are a feature derived from classical lore on proportion. Were these one-fifth the width of vertical stems and so a part of the Vitruvius mystique? In any case, these decisions of Feliciano left him vulnerable, although in one instance, the K, he was successful. In stretching K into a square format Feliciano showed genuine imagination. He produced an interesting letter, which depended on his ability as a calligrapher, but not a letter that a carver could have used. Other instances are less happy, for example, letter D (Fig. 6). Feliciano believed he could stretch this form into a square but, as is clear, his thin transversals left him without a chance to succeed. In letter T, Feliciano pointed the two serifs, initial and terminal to the transversal, toward the opposite juncture of the main-stroke with the base line, and this spark of personal inspiration gave a banal physiognomy, much as if the Mona Lisa should be cross-eyed. Feliciano aranged to get Z into a square but left it in a spavined condition.

Curiously, Feliciano made an acceptable R (in fact two of them) and explained that the *soprascripta* of R was in great part determined by P. It was the tail or *coda* of R that proved to be difficult, and

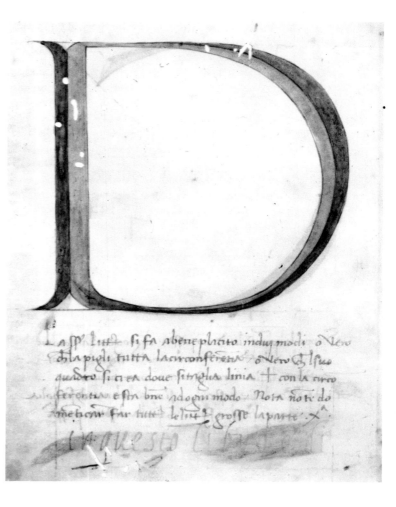

Fig. 6. The D of Felice Feliciano ca. 1460.
Biblioteca Vaticana, Rome.

Feliciano declared that it could not be perfectly achieved by the compass. He was undoubtedly correct in this view, and explained further that it was necessary to experiment many times in order to draw a coda well. His alphabet survives as a monument to a losing struggle with Vitruvius, the compass, and the ancient Roman inscription letter.

The next treatise on constructed letters and the first to be rendered on wood-blocks and printed was by Damiano da Moyle, published at Parma in 1480. This author preferred a proportion of one to twelve in stem width to height, a relationship which may also be devised from Vitruvius "On Symmetry": "The mathematicians, however, maintaining a different view, have said that the perfect number is six, because this number is composed of integral parts which are suited numerically to their method of reckoning. . . . finally, twelve, being composed of the two simple integers, is called double (Book 3, Chapter 1, No. 5)." The da Moyle alphabet presented letters A, C, D, G, H, M, N, O, Q, and V in the square and inscribed circle, but differing formats explained thirteen other letters. Da Moyle also used a 45° diagonal to establish the stress angles in O and Q, thus perpetuating Feliciano's gross misinterpretation. Details in some of da Moyle's letters were described in the arbitrary terms of the ruler, which was neither Vitruvius nor inscription calligraphy. The transversals of his E ended on seven, six, and eight of a twelve-unit division of the square. Da Moyle forced his D wide, nearly square, and this letter is more acceptable than Feliciano's D.

Da Moyle's uninspired alphabet had about it a measure of consistency for which the author deserves full credit. Cut on blocks, da Moyle's alphabet was an expression of the limitations of this medium. Compass skills of this period are best observed in original manuscripts, and the second such expression devoted to Roman capitals is the anonymous Newberry manuscript dated some time before 1500. From this manuscript alphabet letter R (Fig. 7) demonstrates the manner in which original calligraphic serifs were interpreted by an individual skilled in the use of the compass. As may be observed, the coda of R, which disturbed Feliciano, is in this example delineated by intersecting compass curves of very large radii. This extended effort did not improve the tail. The letters in the Newberry manuscript are sturdy, with a proportion of one to nine in stem width to height. Millard Meiss reminds us that this too may derive from a classical proportion, the Platonic as outlined in the *Timaeus*. Presumably the author of the Newberry manuscript capitals would have known of this. The Newberry alphabet is unique in its clarity of intention but its apparent sophistication should not blind anyone to the fact that its letters are, in the view of the veteran calligrapher James Hayes, ugly. Few would care to dissent.

The author of the Newberry capitals omitted the square and inscribed circle but this usage was restored in a printed treatise by Luca Pacioli, a mathematician who had published the best known algebra of the period, *Summa de arithmetica, geometria, proportione et proportionalita*, in Venice in 1494. Capitals drawn by Pacioli were a part of *Divina proportione*, a work otherwise devoted to polygons, solids, and a ratio known as the golden section, and published in Venice in 1509. Pacioli used the square and inscribed circle in all of his letter structures excepting B and S (no Z was printed). Like a good teacher Pacioli presented a short text of explanation with each letter in the prescribed manner. The first sentence of most of these texts proceeded in the manner of that accompanying letter I: "This letter is made from the circle and the square and its thickness must be one-ninth; so that it is easier to make than others."

Thus Pacioli also used the proportion found in the Newberry letters. There are other similarities between the two alphabets; the two R's are practically identical, including the use of large compass curves to form the tail. Although Pacioli stretched his D into a square with moderate success, his alphabet, in terms of a successful meshing of the Vitruvius lore with observation (a task in which he might have been expected to excel), is as coarsely pedantic as any other. Pacioli's B (Fig. 9) demonstrates that units of nine widths should suffice as well as any other to explain the bowls of this letter so

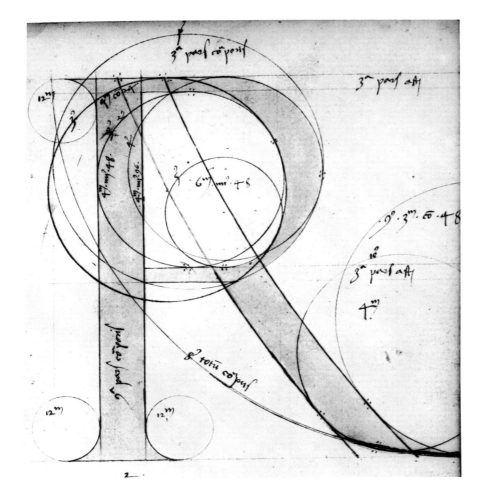

Fig. 7. Letter R from Anonymous Newberry dated prior to 1500. The
Newberry Library, Chicago.

subtly achieved in many Roman inscriptions. In placing *Divina
proportione* in its proper historical niche, mathematics historian Carl B.
Boyer states in *A History of Mathematics* (1968), that the letters are
noteworthy for their excellence. It is to be hoped that some other way
can be found to honor Pacioli.

Other methods of constructing Roman capitals followed. Sigismondo Fanti produced the next version in his *Theorica et practica de
modo scribendi*, published in Venice in 1514. Another was published by
Francesco Torniello in Milan in 1517, *Opera del Modo de Fare le
Littere Maiuscole Antique*. Albrecht Dürer's well-known version of the
Roman capitals appeared in *Underweysung der Messung* (Nürnberg,
1525). Dürer presented alternatives in proportions embodied in the
letters and details of form, describing three differing A's. His approach
to the Roman capitals was perhaps more subtle than some others,
although he extolled the virtues of the compass as a tool. Still another
constructed alphabet was presented by Giovam Baptista Verini in his
Luminario of 1526. Verini's method was strong in compass theory and
his instructions were fairly complete.

Geofroy Tory's constructed alphabets appeared in the famous
Champ Fleury: L'art et science de la proportion des letterres (Paris, 1529).
Tory followed the Vitruvius-Leonardo line of thought in relating
the human figure to the square and inscribed circle. He also attempted
to relate the human figure to the capital letters and the square and
inscribed circle, going so far as to draw faces in O and OI combined.
In constructing the capitals Tory used a grid system of one hundred
squares. Thus his central proportion was one to ten in stem width to
height—derived from the nine Muses with Apollo added. Tory not
only attempted to relate ancient capital letters with Vitruvius but
threw in generous portions of classical mythology and any other
idea that came to hand. Here is his commentary on letter Q:

> This letter Q is the only one of all the letters that goes below
> the lowest line, and I have never been able to find a man who
> could tell me the reason therefor; but I will tell it and set it down

in writing. I have thought and meditated so much on the shape of these Attic letters that I have discovered that the Q extends below the line because he does not allow himself to be written in a complete word without his trusty comrade and brother V [U], and to show that he wishes to have him by his side, he embraces him with his tail from below, as I shall draw him hereafter, in his turn.

Stanley Morison, in *Fra Luca De Pacioli* (1933), mentioned Tory's "insistence upon the importance of his caballistic abracadabra." Although Tory vented his scorn on the constructed alphabets of Fanti, Arrighi, Dürer, and Pacioli (accusing the latter of stealing his letters from Leonardo da Vinci) there is nothing particularly distinguished about his own.

The search for the perfect letter form went on into the sixteenth century and writing master manuals included some graphic representation of the ancient capitals with or without compass marks or texts of instruction. The last effort to be reproduced here (Fig. 8) is the R from the manuscript alphabet by Giovanbattista Palatino, the celebrated scribe and author of the writing manual *Libro nuovo etc.* (Rome, 1540). This manuscript version of constructed capitals exists in the Berlin Kunstbibliothek (Ms. OS5280) and James Wardrop's date of ca. 1550 is approximate: the manuscript and letters seem to have been assembled over a period of time. In Palatino's manuscript R the circle and inscribed square is still in evidence although obscured by the extended play of the compass. Palatino's effort, still echoing Vitruvius, brings us to the date of Cresci's debut in Rome. In all of the compass alphabets from Feliciano to Palatino we can observe the same symmetrical treatment of bowls and that identical treatment of serifs which, shrivelled, stiffened, and deprived of calligraphic grace, mark these static *sylloge*.

Giovan Francesco Cresci would have none of this, and instead advocated a return to the study of ancient inscription letters. It is not

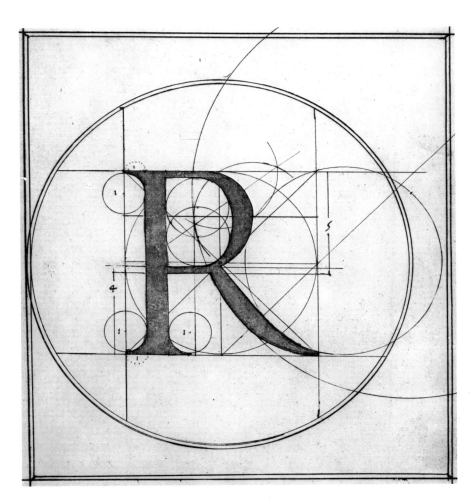

Fig. 8. Palatino's manuscript R ca. 1550.
Kunstbibliothek, Berlin.

known how many compass methods Cresci had seen. In his *Essemplare* facsimile, A. S. Osley has indicated that in *L'Idea* (Milan, 1622), a posthumous publication by Cresci's son, Cresci stated that Dürer might have avoided errors of proportion had he seen Roman inscriptions. Of course he had, in visits to Italy before Cresci was born. The discorso in *Essemplare* contains several well-chosen remarks directed to the authors of compass alphabets: "And in drawing every curve of each letter they make more circles than a sphere for the most part contains." Cresci's summation is even better: "I have come to the conclusion that if Euclid, the prince of geometry, returned to this world of ours, he would never find that the curves of the letters could, by means of circles made with compasses, be constructed according to the proportion and style of the ancient letters."

While Cresci disposed of the constructed alphabets in his *Essemplare* essay it is apparent that he recognized that the 1560 alphabet which he presented in argument was not the perfect case for ancient letters. The conclusion must be drawn that in the decade between *Essemplare* and *Il perfetto scrittore* Cresci became more impressed with the fine detail imbedded in classical inscriptions and less impressed with his own contribution. It must not be concluded that the Trajan inscription was the only set of letters that Cresci admired, but he did cite these letters in *Essemplare* and in *Il perfetto scrittore*. In the latter, the Trajan letters were mentioned in the dedication to Cardinal Salviati and in the discourse on capital letters.

The Trajan inscription appears at the base of a column erected in Rome in A.D. 113 to commemorate Emperor Trajan's victories on the frontier of the Danube. (Curiously, the last two of its six lines have never been translated properly.) Most of the larger letters of the inscription measure about $4\frac{1}{2}$ inches vertical. It is interesting to note that the Cresci letters seen here are actually larger than the letters of the Trajan inscription, measuring about $4\frac{7}{8}$ inches vertical. The only copy to derive from the Renaissance inquiry was that made by Leopardo Antonozzi, and published in *De caratteri* (Rome, 1638). Cresci's praise for them constitutes, therefore, a somewhat lonely stand in his

time. More contemporary views have tended to confirm his judgment on the excellence of the Trajan letters.

Modern interest in the Trajan letters chiefly stems from the work of William Lethaby, Edward Johnston, and Eric Gill in London around the turn of this century. That part of their significant calligraphic movement that concerned inscription forms was based on a plaster copy of the Trajan column deriving from a metal cast ordered by Napoleon III, and acquired by the Victoria and Albert Museum in London in 1864. Neither Napoleon III nor the syndics of the Victoria and Albert Museum seem to have had the slightest interest in the inscription, and it is generally held that the bas-reliefs spiralling the grand monument provided the principal motivation in the chain of events.

Thus the Trajan letters came to be "discovered" again not in Rome but in the Victoria and Albert Museum. Lethaby, the school man, and Johnston, the scholar and calligrapher, generally deferred to Eric Gill and Percy Smith in matters pertaining to inscription forms, but it was Lethaby, writing an editor's preface to Johnston's famous book *Writing & Illuminating, & Lettering* (London, 1906), who outlined the methods employed by Roman inscription writers:

> The Roman characters, which are our letters to-day, although their earlier forms have only come down to us cut in stone, must have been formed by incessant practice with a flat, stiff brush, or some such tool. The disposition of the thicks and thins, and the exact shape of the curves, must have been settled by an instrument used rapidly; I suppose, indeed, that most of the great monumental inscriptions were designed *in situ* by a master writer, and only cut in by the mason, the cutting being merely a fixing, as it were, of the writing, and the cut inscriptions must always have been intended to be completed by painting.

There seemed few who were willing to heed Lethaby's statement. James Mosley has pointed out, in "Trajan Revived" in *Alphabet* (1964), that even before the publication of Johnston's book a new round of compass alphabets had started in being. These inherited the same defects to be seen in efforts from the fifteenth and sixteenth centuries. Even the great Stanley Morison, writing in *Fra Luca de Pacioli*, the splendid Grolier Club édition of 1933, stated: "According to the most authoritative of modern students of epigraphy, Emil Hübner, it is obvious that the more elegant inscriptions were drawn or painted with aid of the rule and compass."

Although Lethaby's statement was correct and Morison's incorrect, proof of the earlier assertion was not forthcoming for lack of original research on the Trajan inscription letters in Rome. The Victoria and Albert cast was a rather gross interpretation of the subtle detail of the original, but between Emil Hübner's study of about 1880, *Exempla Scripturae Epigraphicae Latinae*, and 1935 the only recorded study of the Trajan letters was represented by four crude rubbings obtained by Ernst Detterer, who had earlier studied briefly with Johnston at Ditchling, and a companion in 1922.

Thus while the Trajan letters became popular in the schools and letter trades of London the inscription in Rome remained undisturbed. After Antonozzi's published study of the Trajan letters in 1638, the first accurate rendition of them was produced by Fr. Edward M. Catich, who in the late 1930s made tracings from a scaffold, and finally published them in *The Trajan Inscriptions in Rome* (Davenport, Iowa, 1961). Catich's studies of the *ductus* of Imperial letters are found in his *The Origin of the Serif* (Davenport, Iowa, 1968).

Even one skilled in the handling of the ancient calligraphic brush will not find the Catich theory easy. It is clear, however, that Lethaby's "master writer" was just that. A key part of the Catich paleography lies in his revelation that some vertical stems of letters are not quite vertical and indeed could not have been ruled or measured, a myth which seems to have been particularly difficult to dislodge not only in the thinking of Vitruvius addicts of an earlier day but in our own.

The Catich interpretation of the brush strokes of Imperial B is seen here with Pacioli's constructed B, and a drawing of the larger B found in the Trajan inscription, this last showing how the Roman carver interpreted the brush-written letter in V-cut incisions (Figs. 9–11). Since our understanding of these matters has only recently been advanced by Catich, it seems even more certain that no one in Renaissance times understood serif structure or the nature of its origin. The 1570 alphabet of Cresci and the fine inscriptions emerging from the *bottegas* of Italy were then in part skilled imitations.

The drift in Cresci's thinking toward a closer allegiance to the classical letter is first traced through his selection of proportion. He gave up the one to eight proportion seen in his 1560 letters for a proportion that is reasonably close to that existing in the Trajan letters. Of course the proportions found in the Trajan letters vary from

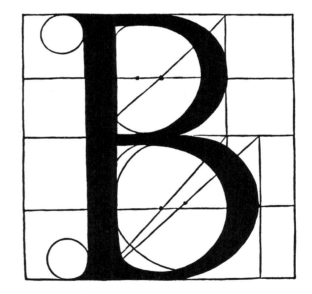

Fig. 9. Pacioli's B in *De divina proportione*,
1509. Grolier Club facsimile,
New York, 1933.

one to less than nine through one to more than eleven. The proportion of Cresci's 1570 letters seems something like one to ten and a half. Cresci was never rigid on proportion, believing that a number of ratios could suit differing needs, so in the drawing of the *Il perfetto scrittore* letters the move toward the Trajan letters seems deliberate.

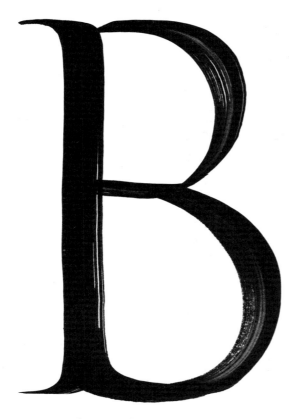

Fig. 10. Brush-written B courtesy
Fr. Edward M. Catich, St. Ambrose
College, Davenport, Iowa.

Cresci significantly gave up the stiff vertical serifs on the horizontal stroke of T, and changed these in the 1570 letters to forms more like those deriving from calligraphy. Median transversals on the E and F of the 1570 alphabet show some modest change along this line too. Cresci apparently had intimate knowledge of the stress angle of O and Q. In his 1560 letters he turned this angle slightly counterclockwise and gave reasons for the move. In the 1570 letters O and Q possess angles that are almost as vertical as those found in the Trajan letters.

The anatomy of M and N deserve special mention. In the Cresci M presented here, shoulder serifs are present where none is seen on the Trajan letters. This latter treatment in classical inscriptions is by no means standard. In inscription M's before the date of Trajan blunt endings are usually seen at the shoulders, a natural meeting of vertical and diagonal brush strokes. But occasionally serifs are seen as in inscription no. 45 in the classic collection by A. and J. Gordon, *Album of Dated Latin Inscriptions* (Berkeley, 1958–65). After a rough date of A.D. 200 serifs are more frequently seen on the shoulders of M's but the treatment shows wide variation. It may be said that the form of shoulder serif used by Cresci was the version that won out in the Renaissance, a stabilization of form taking place before Cresci was born. The Trajan form, without serifs, is extinct in the Renaissance.

There are also changes in N through the years. There is little to comment on in the serif initiating the right stem, since this feature was one of the stable parts of classical letter anatomy. Serifs atop the left stem are certainly seen before the date of the Trajan column, most notably perhaps in the Gaius Caesar inscription of A.D. 1 and in the epitaph of C. Iulius Eros, a baker, dating A.D. 11. Again there was a wide variety of treatments for the left shoulder of N, at times full serifs on a bias directed to the diagonal, and at other times a mere suggestion of brush strokes initiating the diagonal. These various serifs of the left shoulder of N are increasingly seen after the Trajan date and may be said to be a stable feature of N before 1500. Both verticals in Cresci's N were thinned down in comparison to these same strokes in the Trajan N's. This too was a standard practice before Cresci's time. This is not to say that the Roman calligraphers were mistaken, but in black and white versions of N the letter benefits from the thinning of these strokes.

Paleography on the rare letters in Latin inscriptions is relative to the orthography of Latin and Italian. In neither language was K an essential letter, and in Latin inscriptions K was employed to spell such Greek words as *kalendis*, the first day of the month. Form too followed Greek kappas, and in early Roman inscriptions this character featured short curved arms, and a total physiognomy that was almost ludicrous in its environment of sturdy Roman letters. Throughout the history of the Roman inscription letter there are almost as many solutions to the anatomy of this Greek import as appearances. It is difficult to point to any of these as the origin of the Renaissance K, which is in no measure more frequently seen than earlier, since Latin was the epitaph language and the employment of Italian would not have increased the population of K's anyway.

A K in the epitaph of antipope John XXIII in the Florence Baptistry, carved by Donatello and Michelozzo in the 1420s, shows curves on both arms of K. Presumably the angle-armed K became standard in the latter half of the fifteenth century, but apparently the method of joining the arms to the stem did not, for in the theoretical compass treatments several methods were shown. Cresci seems to have preferred the K's of Feliciano, da Moyle, and Arrighi, wherein the arms just touched the stem, rather than the K's drawn by Verini or Pacioli, wherein the authors planted the arms firmly into the stem.

The Y too was rare in Roman inscriptions and is seen in many variations. A rather perfectly modern Y, in proportion quite like Cresci's seen here, appears in no. 27 of the Gordon albums, the epitaph of PINYTVS, dated after A.D. 14. Among many other versions of Y created by Roman calligraphers was the upsilon, with two great curved arms rising above the other letters. Both forms of Y were preserved in the Renaissance. In San Pancrazio (1467) in Florence, Alberti used an angular Y, but the upsilon form is seen in the PRESBYTER on the tomb of Cardinal D'Albret in Rome (1465) and in the XYSTO inscribed on the tomb of Cardinal Alanus (d. 1474) existing in Rome.

Fig. 11. Drawing of the large B in the Trajan inscription in Rome, A.D. 113. D. M. Anderson.

Feliciano and most of the other authors of compass alphabets did not include the upsilon form, although Verini did. In Verini's version the curved arms did not rise above the height of other letters. Arrighi in the 1523 alphabet reproduced here presented both angular and curved forms of Y and thereafter in their turn other writing masters, Tagliente, Palatino, and Yciar, did the same. Cresci followed this practice in his 1560 alphabet. His upsilon form, in exotic confrontation with Z, is seen in Fig. 3. Cresci remarked that along with S and the tails of R and Q, this form of Y required considerable skill and experience, but this was his last comment on upsilon Y, and he did not include this form in his 1570 letters. It was a marvelous form, still, out of place in the environment of Trajan forms.

Early in their history the Latin speakers threw zeta out of their alphabet because it was not needed. Later they had to put it back in to spell Greek names. An early Z, perfectly well formed as we know it, appears in the Gordon collections, spelling Zethus and dated in the first years of the Christian era. When rarely used, Z was often wider than square. Renaissance theoreticians generally found that it was eminently suited to the square of Vitruvius, although some alphabets show Z wider than square, as in the dubious letter of Nicolas Jenson's types. As noted, Feliciano drew a miserable Z and the Z's of Arrighi, Tagliente, Palatino, and Yciar are pitiful, suggesting that good models were not plentiful. Besides that, they copied each other. In comparison, Cresci's 1560 design of Z is a superb achievement. In the Z of *Il perfetto scrittore* Cresci corrected the overbite of the top transversal and made the letter more vertical. It is difficult to fault his thinking here; this letter seems to suit the others well.

One of Creci's special concerns was the letter Q. He wrote that the true and correct length of Q's tail is a little less than twice the width of the oval part of the letter. He stated that such a correct Q could be found in a set of small capitals on page xxxxiii of *Essemplare*, but the Q there does not possess a tail of this dimension. Cresci's view on his larger 1560 Q (Fig. 3) is also expressed in *Essemplare*: "But, in my large alphabet, I have been unable to allow the tail of Q its proper length because the frame of the page was too narrow. If I had wanted to make a frame larger than the others in order to do this, I should have thrown the whole book out of proportion."

Actually the 1560 Q is beautifully proportioned, as may be seen, with a total length quite precisely twice the diameter of the oval. In this kind of comparison the tail of Cresci's 1560 Q is more generous than either Q in the Trajan inscription.

But this reduction must have preyed on Cresci's mind in the ten-year period separating the two manuals, for in *Il perfetto scrittore* he jettisoned the principle of unity of format and prepared a very lengthy rendition of Q's tail. It goes on and on. This forced Aureri to prepare a very large block, $7\frac{1}{4}$ inches high and about $18\frac{1}{2}$ inches wide, not including border material. To say the least, there are clumsy aspects to this presentation. In neither the dark nor the light printing did Q and R fall in the middle of a signature, so that the block was cut in half for printing, narrowing the possibility that Q's tail could be presented without a kink in it. In any case, a portion of Q's tails are seized in the binding, and this presents a rather formidable problem in facsimile reproduction. In all black and white reproductions of Cresci's 1570 capitals it has been necessary to redraw the tail of Q, and one well-known museum published a version of the letters with Q's tail shortened. In this facsimile edition of Cresci's 1570 capitals the versions of Q are tinged with imperfection but not seriously curtailed.

The capitals in *Il perfetto scrittore* are, in vertical dimension, almost twice that of Cresci's 1560 letters. It cannot be discounted that Cresci wanted his 1570 letters to equal or exceed the scale of the Trajan letters, but it seems better to assume that the larger dimension afforded Cresci a proper outlet for his aesthetic views and the accurate presentation of these in every detail. Some of Cresci's strokes are quite fragile. The lower curve of D's bowl is delicately honed, and for some it may seem that the anatomy of R is too refined at the mid-arm juncture. But it is obvious that these details are clearly shown and in these larger letters Cresci was able to reveal what he wanted his readers to see.

This concern with scale and proper presentation no doubt evolved from the technical problems of inking and printing: "And in my attempt to keep the field black, the excessive amount of ink needed for the press in some cases distorts the capitals." In the letters seen here there is little evidence of the distortion that Cresci feared, although the dangers may be observed in wood-engraved letters from Arrighi's time onward. Arrighi's little colophon (Fig. 1) had to be retouched for this facsimile because the ampersand had filled in. Cresci's remarks are taken from his discorso in *Il perfetto scrittore*, prepared before the act of printing; it is reasonable to assume that he had learned his lesson from some other publication, for instance, from two engraved alphabetic specimen plates in *Essemplare*. One of these plates was devoted to an elegantly designed example of the Roman minuscule with the m possessing a vertical dimension of $\frac{1}{4}$ inch. The other plate was principally devoted to small Roman capitals only a shade larger. These were vulnerable to the excess inking of the day, as extant copies clearly demonstrate. Even the few copies of *Il perfetto scrittore* available in the world show a wide variation in the inking. In the Victoria and Albert copy Cresci's black-field alphabet is almost completely black, while these same areas in a Newberry Library copy are muddy with a deterioration of the ink. It is clear that in this period very large relief surfaces were difficult to print.

Cresci recognized this, and did not want to see his alphabet printed with a black field. It could not be avoided, apparently, and he consented to it only "to satisfy certain friends whose wishes I could not slight," naming no names. Cresci printed the grey-field alphabet for himself. "The requirement of less ink for the field of the capitals makes them stand out more clearly and in greater relief without their lines being in any way distorted." The first part of this statement seems to constitute evidence that Cresci was aware that the white-on-black alphabet, with its dazzling contrasts, interfered with perception—a view in which he would now receive support. In any case the alphabet of the grey field is preferable and the double printing of the Cresci-Aureri blocks is indeed unique and belongs to

Cresci. As can be observed, Cresci's alphabet of the gray field reveals the texture of brass wires used in the laid moulds employed in the hand-production methods of papermaking of 1570, before the development of paper by wove moulds in England by the middle of the eighteenth century. The slightly engraved quality of Cresci's paper undoubtedly complicated the printing problem. Lighter inking in the grey-field alphabets was satisfactory, but in the black-field inkings the laid mould texture was never quite hidden. So much the better for students of papermaking, even though it was a problem for Cresci and the printers of his *casa*.

The specimen blocks of *Essemplare* were surrounded by fussy border material. Curiously, in *Il perfetto scrittore* Cresci used decorative borders around the alphabet of the black field but presented the alphabet of the grey field plain. In his essay Cresci did not explain this, but we do know that the white-on-black letters were printed to please a sponsor and can presume that the border material too was meant to please this anonymous benefactor. The Newberry Library possesses two editions of Cresci's 1570 blocks with differing border material and it is difficult to choose the most banal of them, since each has strong points.

Perhaps in Cresci's type pages there is another answer to the omission of border. The *discorsi* and dedicatory pages were set in wide measure (49 picas) to match the width of the blocks. And these front matter pages appear, exept for a wood cut initial, in an unbroken shape without indentations. Clearly Cresci had in mind here matching type bodies to the shape of the letter blocks, a fundamentally sound intention followed in this facsimile.

It cannot be said that Cresci's sensible views won the day. His emphatic rejection of the compass as a proper tool in creating Roman letters was countermanded by his most gifted student, Luca Horfei da Fano, and more banal compass alphabets followed. Rather, Cresci's aesthetic concerns make him a man for our own times. In the discourse in *Il perfetto scrittore* he said, "And let no one marvel if on measuring the capitals (as, for example, the A) he finds that the transversal is thinner than the first (left) stroke, for if it were as thick, it would, being shorter, seem even thicker."

In the commentary seen in translation here Cresci stated that he had hoped to include the rules for drawing the ancient letters he admired. The reason given for the omission was lack of space. The better reason is that Cresci's views prevented his inclusion of such rules. If there is a content of maturity in the treatise of *Il perfetto scrittore* it surely resides in this tribute:

> These ancient capitals are so noble in themselves that I think one can truly say that they provide the opportunity for infinite study. In this regard, I should like to cite by way of example the art of painting: Although there are rules and proportions to assure that in painting a beautiful figure its various parts are in harmony, nevertheless, there are still some painters who are so studious in their craft and so favoured by heaven in their art that despite rules, they will infuse more life, energy and grace into their figures than will another no matter how good a painter he may be. I repeat, then, that the possibility of study in these capitals is so limitless that one should not attempt to lay down precise rules about them or any other matter which someone, as I have shown by my example, could surpass in grace and beauty.

Donald M. Anderson, November, 1970

LIST OF REFERENCES

Antonozzi, Leopardo. *De caratteri*. Rome, 1638.

Catich, Edward M. *The Origin of the Serif*. Davenport, Iowa, 1968.

———. *The Trajan Inscription in Rome*. Davenport, Iowa, 1961.

Damiano da Moyle. *Alphabetum*. Parma, 1480.

Dürer, Albrecht. *Underweysung der Messung*. Nürnberg, 1525.

Fanti, Sigismondo. *Theorica et practica de modo scribendi*. Venice, 1514.

Feliciano, Felice. *Felice Feliciano Veronese: Alphabetum Romanum*. ed. Giovanni Mardersteig. Verona, 1960.

Gordon, Arthur and Joyce. *Album of Dated Latin Inscriptions*. 4 vols. Berkeley, Cal., 1958–65.

Johnston, Edward. *Writing & Illuminating, & Lettering*. London, 1906.

Juan de Yciar. *Arte subtilissima*. Saragossa, 1550.

Hercolani, Giuliantonio. *Lo scrittor' utile*. Bologna, 1574.

Hübner, Emil. *Exempla Scripturae Epigraphicae Latinae*. Berlin, 1885.

Kristeller, Paul. *Andrea Mantegna*. Berlin, 1902.

Ludovico degli Arrighi. *Il modo de temperare le penne*. Venice. 1523.

———. *La operina*. Rome, 1522.

Morison, Stanley. *Fra Luca de Pacioli*. New York, 1933.

Mosley, James. "Trajan Revived" in *Alphabet*. Vol. 1, Birmingham, 1964.

Osley, A. S. *Giovan Francesco Cresci, Examplare di Più Sorti Lettere*. London, 1968.

Paciolo, Luca. *Divina Proportione . . .* Venice, 1509.

———. *Summa de arithmetica, geometria, proportioni et proportionalita*. Venice, 1494.

Palatino, Giovanbattista. *Libro nuovo . . .* Rome, 1540.

Torniello, Francesco. *Opera del Modo de Fare le Littere Maiuscole Antique . . .* Milan, 1517.

Tory, Jeofroy. *L'art et science de la proportion des letterres*. Paris, 1529.

Verini, Giovam Baptista. *Luminario*. Tusculano (on Lake Garda), 1526.

A RENAISSANCE ALPHABET

DISCORSO DELLE MAIVSCOLE
antiche Romane.

Vanto ſia neceſſaria l'intelligenza delle maiuſcole antiche Romane a coloro, che uogliono peruenire alla eccellenza della pratti ca, che a buono ſcrittore ſi ricerca nello ſcriuere, quelli che in cio ſtudieranno, & che il grado del eccellente ſcrittore aſſeguir deſiderarăno, la preſente mia opera(credo)glie ne darà piu chiara & fortiſſima teſtimonianza, che cö tutte le parole ſopra cio poteſſi eſplicare. Concioſia che uedute l'opere di tutti quelli che fin qui hanno fatto profeſſione di queſto eſſercitio, ſi vedrà ma nifeſtamente la poca prattica & il poco giuditio, che hanno hauuto in queſt'arte per mancamento della luce di queſte maiuſco le, le quali in vero ſono il fundamento di tutta la theorica, & prattica dello ſcriuer eccellente ogni qualità di lettera, maſſi me della lettera antica tonda, & cancellareſca antica. L'animo mio era di darne fuori le loro regole ſecondo il modo che gli antichi vſorono ; ma conſiderato che il volume di queſt'opera non lo comportaua, ho dato fuori ſolamente la forma di det te maiuſcole. Percioche quelli pochi che a queſta eccellenza uorranno attendere, eſſendo le dette maiuſcole di molta grandezza, & condotte in quella nettezza che deſiderar ſi poſſa, piu facilmente potranno ſtudiare le loro proportioni, & col tempo, per l'eſſempio loro, trouar il modo d'inten derle, & di condurle molto bene alla ſua perfettione. Et perche forſe alcuno potrebbe dire, che hauendo eſſi le regole che inſegnaſſero il modo di for mar dette maiuſcole, in pochi giorni ſi ſarebbono facilmente imparate, non negherò io che non haueſſero aperta un poco di via, & data qualche luce, ma dico bene, che quanto al perfettamente, & preſto imparar, s'ingannano. Perche hauendo io gia eſperimentato con inſegnar le dette regole ad alcuni miei ingegnoſi diſcepoli, ci hanno con tutto cio ſpeſo lo ſtudio di molti meſi et anni, innanzi che habbiano poſſuto metter in prattica a tal regole, & acquiſtarne vna mano eſperta in formarle per prattica con la penna. Queſte maiuſcole antiche ſono in ſe tanto nobili, che a me pare che ſi poſſa dire ueramēte, che portano in loro ſtudio infinito, il che ſi puo conſiderare per uia d'eſſempio, che ſi come anchora nell'arte della pittura ſono regole & proportioni per dipinger vna bella figura, che moſtri bene i ſuoi membri, & che ſe le conuengono, nientidimeno fra li pittori ſe ne trouano alcuni, che ſono tanto ſtudioſi, inclinati, & fauoriti dal cielo in tal arte, che non oſtanti le dette regole, alle loro figure daranno piu viuacità, piu forza, & piu gratia, che non farà un'al tro per buon pittor che ſia. Però di nuouo dico, che lo ſtudio di queſte maiuſcole è infinito, perche non biſogna far diſſegno di dar regole ſopra qual ſi uo glia materia tanto ben finite, che alcuno, per l'eſſempio di ſopra detto, non le poſſa auanzare in qualche coſa di maggior gratia, & bellezza. Ogni ſtu dioſo ſcrittore adunque che di queſte maiuſcole ſi dilettarà, con tutto che haueſſe le mie regole, ouer che per miſurar l'altezze, & larghezze delle linee, & delli corpi, & altre particularità di dette mie maiuſcole, le ritrouaſſe, ſi come ho fatto io ſopra quelle che ho cauate, & ſtampate dalle forme de li pro prij marmi antichi di Roma, toccherà con mano quanto ſia nobile, & alto, lo ſtudio di dette maiuſcole, & la uerità di tutto quello che diſopra ho detto. Non laſſerò gia, per ſatisfattione di quelli che ſe ne dilettano, & anco per piu cōmune vtile, con la prima cōmodità di dar fuora l'ordine delle rego le ch'io tengo in formar dette maiuſcole, benche prima ſi daranno le regole che conuengono per iſcriuer lettera cancellareſca corrente, per hauerle pri ma di queſt'altre promeſſe. Ne ſi marauigli alcuno, ſe queſt' alfabeto ho poſto ſtampato in queſto libro duplicato, perche ho voluto a ſatisfattione di cer ti amici mei (al bel ingegno & deſiderio de quali non ho poſſuto mācare) ſtamparlo in campo ben nero, perche coſi amauano di veder tal campo. Et per hauer io voluto tener il campo ben nero, per la molta tinta che per queſto effetto alle forme ſi daua, li contorni di dette maiuſcole ſon riuſciti nello ſtam
pare

DISCOURSE ON ANCIENT ROMAN CAPITALS

Translation by Robert J. Rodini

I believe that this work, more than any number of words which I could write on the subject, will give the clearest proof of how necessary a knowledge of ancient Roman capitals is to those who would attain excellence in the art of calligraphy and achieve the reputation of a fine writer. One need only look at the work of all those who have professed accomplishment in this art to see really how little skill and judiciousness they have brought to their work due to their ignorance of these capitals, truly the basis of all theory and practice in the art of excellently writing every type of letter and particularly Roman minuscule and Chancery cursive. I had hoped to supply the rules used by the ancients, but given the limited size of this volume, I have included only the form of the capitals. Since the letters are very large and printed as clearly as one could wish, those few who would achieve excellence in calligraphy will be more easily able to study their proportions and, with time and by their example, come to understand them and to draw them to perfection. Some might well object and say that were they to have the rules teaching the proper manner of forming these capitals, they could easily learn them in a few days. I will not deny that the rules could open the way and give some indication of how to form the letters; but I also say that it is a mistake to think that the rules could teach one quickly and perfectly. Because having myself tried to teach these rules to some of my clever disciples, I found that they still spent many months and years of study before being able to put the rules to use and to acquire from them a hand expert at forming the capitals with a pen. These ancient capitals are so noble in themselves that I think one can truly say that they provide the opportunity for infinite study. In this regard, I should like to cite by way of example the art of painting: although there are rules and proportions to assure that in painting a beautiful figure its various parts are in harmony, nevertheless, there are still some painters who are so studious in their craft and so favored by heaven in their art that despite the rules, they will infuse more life, energy and grace into their figures than will another no matter how good a painter he may be. I repeat, then, that the possibility of study in these capitals is so limitless that one should not attempt to lay down precise rules about them or any other matter which someone, as I have shown by my example, could surpass in grace and beauty. Regardless of what my rules could teach about measuring the height or width of the main-strokes, the bodies and the other details of the capitals, every dedicated calligrapher who appreciates them, were he to find them and print them as I did from the ancient inscriptions on marbles in Rome, would himself experience both the nobility of the study of the capitals and the truth of all that I have said. For the common good and to satisfy those who might derive some pleasure from them, I shall not fail, at the first opportunity, to provide the rules for forming the capitals; but first I shall give those rules pertaining to the writing of Chancery cursive, since I promised them before the others. Nor should anyone marvel at the fact that in this volume I have printed the alphabet in duplicate, because I wished to satisfy certain friends, whose wishes I could not slight, by printing it on a black field since they preferred it that way. And in my attempt to keep the field black, the excessive amount of ink needed for the press in some cases distorted the capitals. Because of this, for my own satisfaction and for the common good, I decided to reprint the alphabet on a grey field so that all could more readily see the perfection and clarity of the lines. The requirement of less ink for the ground of the capitals

pare, in qualche parte offesi. Doue per questo difetto, per satisfattion mia, & per piu cōmune vtilità, ho poi uoluto farlo ristampar in campo bertino, accio che si uegga piu presto da coloro che se ne dilettano, la perfettione & nettezza de i contorni che si richiede di vedere a dette maiuscole, che la bellezza del campo nero, & per la magrezza della tinta che al campo di dette maiuscole si è osseruato di dare nello stamparle, si vedono tanto giusti, netti, & spiccati i loro contorni senza alcuna offensione, che pare a punto che dette maiuscole siano rileuate, & per questa tal cagione ho uoluto stamparlo in tutti dua i modi, per satisfare a i varij gusti delle persone. Ho voluto osseruar ancora in dette maiuscole la sueltezza che ha vsato l'antico, si come per l'epitafio della colōna di Traiano, et altri marmi che in Roma si uedono. Et questa sorte di sueltezza che per le mie maiuscole si puo misurare, mi pare che sia la piu bella & miglior di tutte quante si possono vsare, perche la maiuscola viene a riceuere in se quella maestà & gratia, che desiderar si possa. Habbiano auertenza coloro che le studieranno, di unir con discrettione li corpi con l'haste, con quel giuditio che per le dette mie maiuscole si vede. Et non si marauiglino se trouaranno misurandole, come per l'essempio della maiuscola A. il tratto della sùa trauersa di mezzo esser piu sottile della sua prima asta, perche se tal trauersa si facesse cosi grossa come la sua prima asta, uerrebbe per la cortezza a mostrar all'occhio poi piu grossezza della detta prima asta di detto A. Cosi parimente queste & altre misure, & considerationi s'habbiano nelle aste, & corpi delle maiuscole. B. D. G. T. Q. R. & similmente anco in quelle che non han corpo, perche simil auertenze & considerationi son molto belle, & contentano l'occhio di chi le mira, si come per le maiuscole che nella detta colonna sono scolpite, & per altri marmi di Roma tal considerationi si uedono.

makes them stand out more clearly and in greater relief without their lines being in any way distorted. For this reason, I decided to print the alphabet in both ways and thus satisfy the various tastes of people. I also wanted to preserve in the capitals the thin curvature used in antiquity, as can be seen in the inscription on Trajan's column and on other marbles in Rome. And this type of thin curvature which can be measured in my capitals seems the best and most beautiful of all that can be used because the letter comes to possess the desired majesty and grace.

Let those who would study these capitals be careful to use discretion in joining the body of the letter with the stems and to use the judiciousness which is evident in my own capitals. And let no one marvel if on measuring the capitals (as, for example, the A) he finds that the transversal is thinner than the first (left) stroke, for if it were as thick, it would, being shorter, seem even thicker. Similar and other differences in measurement should be carefully considered in the stems and bodies of the letters B. D. G. T. Q. R. as well as in those letters without bodies. Such considerations please the eye of the beholder, as can be seen in the capitals in Trajan's inscription and in other Roman marbles.

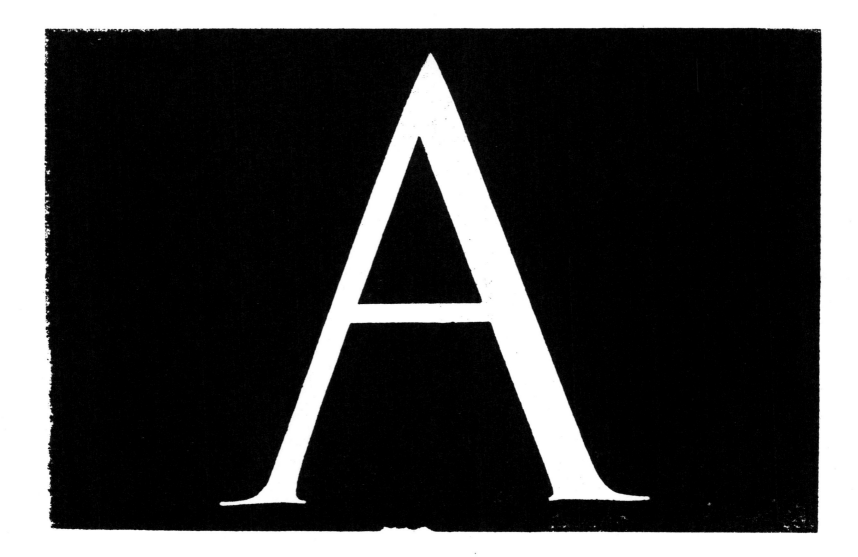

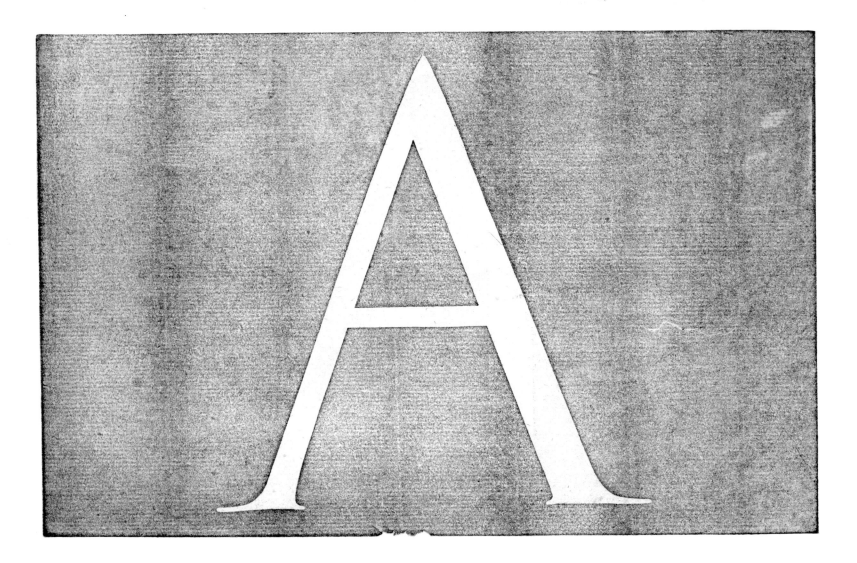

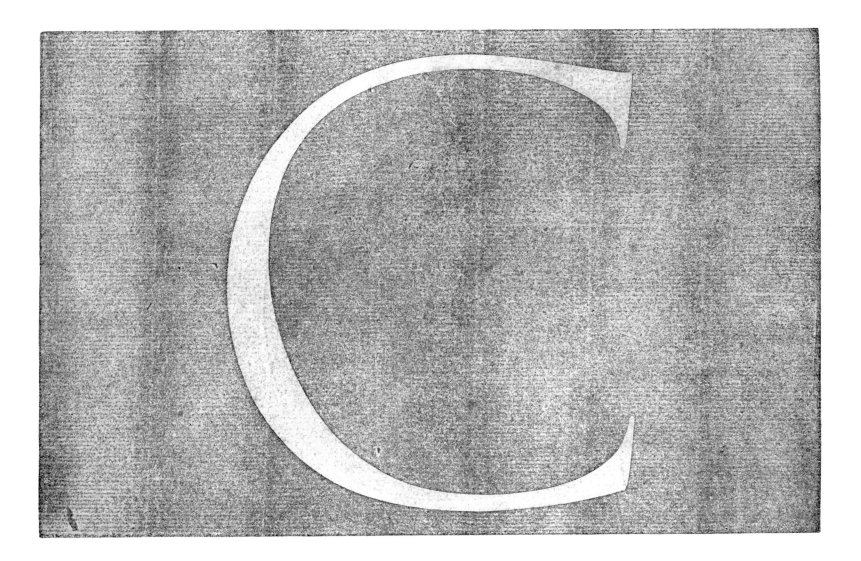

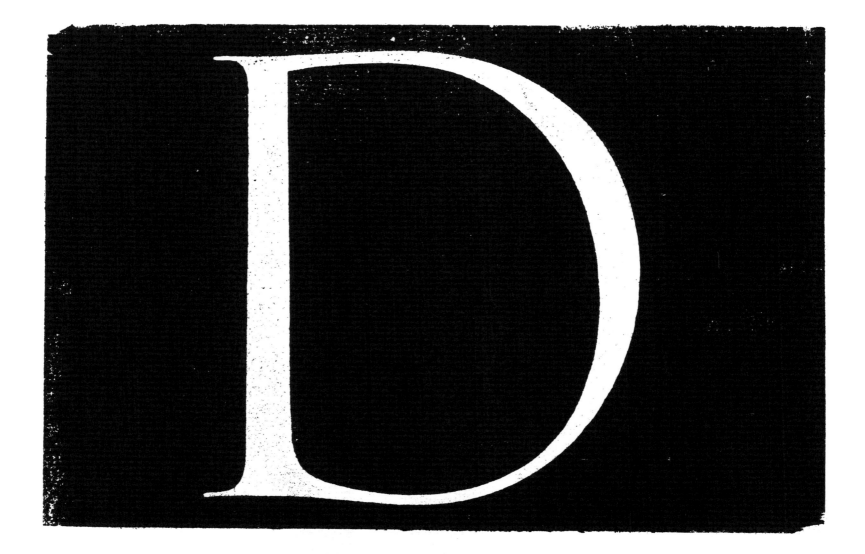

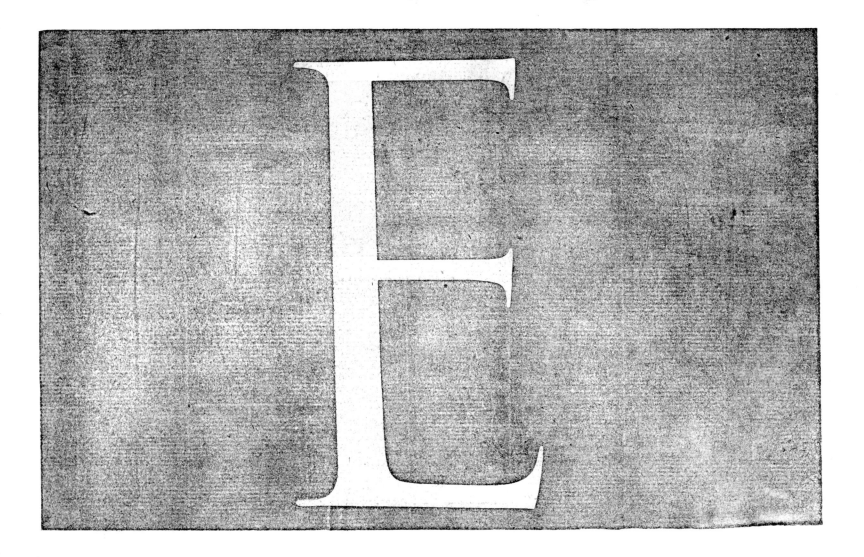

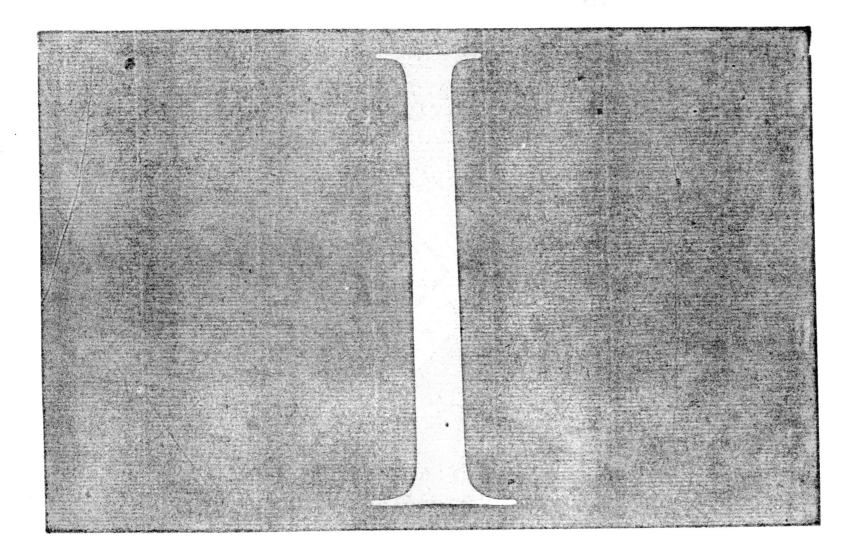

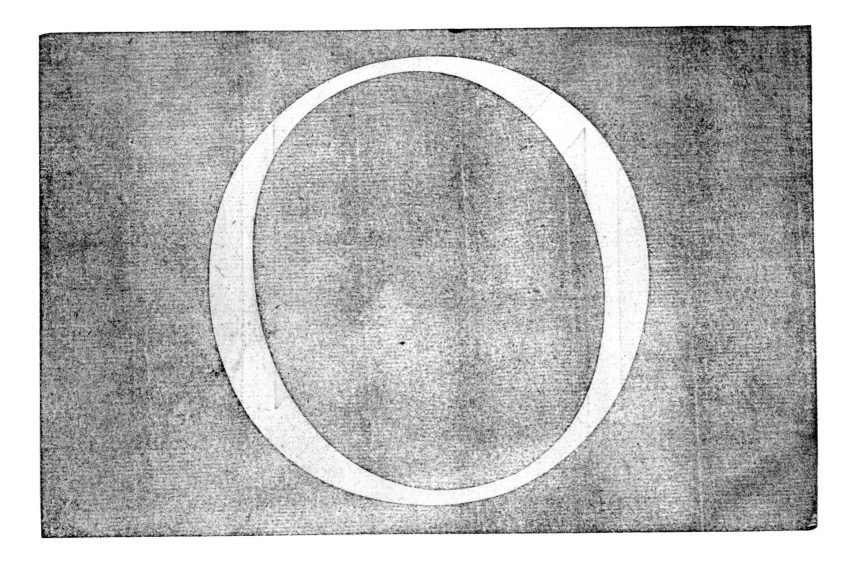

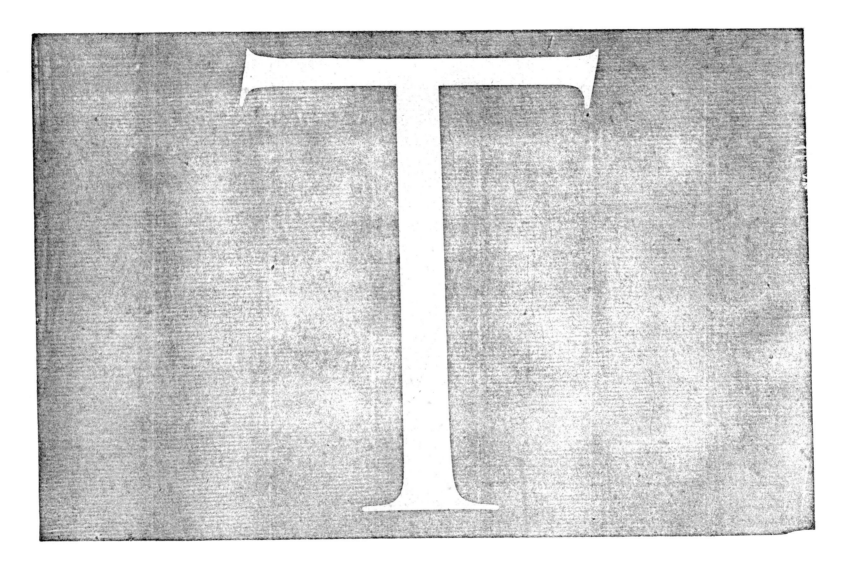